it is *Well* with my *Soul*

This book belongs to:

_____

- - - - - - - - - - - - - - - - - - - -

_____

For I know the plans I have for you

declares the Lord, "plans to prosper

you and not to harm you," plans

to give you hope and a future"

Jeremiah 29:11

Your word is a lamp to my feet

and a light for my path

Psalm 119:105

Trust in the Lord with all your

heart and lean not on your

own understanding

Proverbs 3:5

Therefore, if anyone is in Christ, he
is a new creation; the old has gone,
and the new has come.
2 Corinthians 16:13

Pray without Ceasing

1 Thessalonians 5:17

Be on your guard; stand firm
in the faith; be courageous
— 1 Corinthians 16:13

And whatever you do, do it

heartily, as to the Lord and

not to men.

Colossians 3:23

For where your treasure is,

there will your heart be also.

Luke 12:34

I can do all things through

Christ who strengthens me

Philippians 4:13

My God shall supply all your

needs according to his riches in

glory by Christ Jesus

Philippians 4:19

You keep him in perfect peace

whose mind is stayed on you,

because he trusts in you.

Isaiah 26:3

If any of you lacks wisdom,

let him ask God, who gives

generously to all without reproach,

and it will be given him.

James 1:5

Oh the men would praise the
Lord for his goodness, and for his
wonderful works to the
children of men.

Psalm 107:8

For he satisfies the thirsty and
fills the hungry with good things.
Psalm 107:9

Do not be deceived: God cannot
be mocked. A man reaps
what he sows.
Galatians 6:7

The Lord is my shepherd;

I shall not want

Psalm 23:6

Surely goodness and mercy shall

follow me all the days of my

life, and I shall dwell in the

house of the Lord forever.

Psalm 23:6

And we know that all things

work together for good to them

that love God, to them who are

called according to his purpose

Romans 8:28

What shall we then say to these things? If God is for us who can be against us?

Romans 8:31

In everything give thanks:

for this is the will of God

in Christ Jesus concerning you

to give you hope and a future"

1 Thessalonians 5:18

For God hath not given us the

spirit of fear; but of power, and

of love, and of a sound mind.

2 Timothy 1:7

Jesus answered, "I am the way
and the truth and the life.
no one comes to the Father
except through me."

John 14:6

For all have sinned and fall short of the glory of God.

Romans 3:23

For by grace you have been saved

through faith. And this is not

your own doing; it is the

gift of God.

Ephesians 2:8

I praise you because I am
fearfully and wonderfully made;
your works are wonderful,
I know that full well.

Psalm 139:14

Love the Lord your God with
all your heart and with all your
soul and with all your strength.
Deuteronomy 6:5

Love your neighbour as yourself.

Matthew 22:39

Do not be anxious about
anything, but in every situation,
by prayer and petition, with
thanksgiving present your requests
to God

Philippians 4:6

And the peace of God, which transcends all understanding, will guard your hearts and your minds in Christ Jesus.

Philippians 4:7

Every word of God proves true;

he is a shield to those who

take refuge in him.

Proverbs 30:5

So whether you eat or drink
or whatever you do, do it all for
the glory of God.
1 Corinthians 10:31

In the beginning God created

the heavens and the earth.

Genesis 1:1

The heavens declare the glory
of God; the skies proclaim the
work of His hands

Psalm 19:1

The Lord knows the way

of the righteous, but the way

of the wicked will perish.

Psalm 1:6

...This says the Lord... Fear not,

for I have redeemed you;

I have called you by name,

you are mine

Isaiah 43:11

For my house will be called a

house of prayer for all nations

Isaiah 57:70

You are the light of the

world. A city set on a hill

cannot be hidden.

Matthew 5:14

Let your light shine before men,

that they may see your good deeds

and praise your Father in heaven.

Jeremiah 29:11

Seek ye first the kingdom of
God, and his righteousness;
and all these things shall be
added unto you.
Matthew 6:33

Let the word of Christ

dwell in you richly in

all wisdom.

Colossians 3:16

Jesus Christ is the same yesterday and today and forever.

Hebrews 13:8

They that wait upon the Lord shall

renew their strength; they shall

mount up with wings as eagles; they

shall run and not be weary; and

they shall walk, and not faint.

Isaiah 40:31

Peace I leave with you; my peace
I give you. I do not give to you
as the world gives. Do not let your
hearts be troubled or afraid.

John 14:27

Commit your way to the Lord;

trust in him and he will do this: He

will make your righteous reward

shine like the dawn.

Psalm 37:4

Ask, and you shall receive,

that your joy may be full.

John 16:24b

For God so loved the world that
he gave his only Son, that
whoever believes in him shall not
perish but have eternal life.

John 3:16

Beloved, let us love one another,

for love is of God; and everyone

who loves is born of God and

knows God.

1 John 4:7

Let us think of ways to motivate

one another to acts of love and

good works.

Hebrews 10:24

Whatever is true, whatever is noble,
whatever is right, whatever is pure,
whatever is lovely, whatever is
admirable - if anything is excellent
or praiseworthy - think about
such things.

Philippians 4:8

If they obey and serve him,

They will spend the rest of their

days in prosperity, and their

years in contentment

Job 36:11

Forget the former things; do not

dwell on the past. See, I am

doing a new thing!

to give you hope and a future"

Isaiah 43:18-19a

Let everything that has breath

praise the Lord. Praise the Lord.

Psalm 150:6

For the wages of sin is death,
but the gift of God is eternal
life in Christ Jesus our Lord.

Romans 6:23

Here I am! I stand at the door
and knock. If anyone hears my
voice and opens the door, I will come
in and eat with him.

Revelation 3:20

For it is by grace you have been saved through faith and this not from yourselves, it is the gift of God, not by works, so that no one can boast.

Ephesians 2:8-9

How beautiful on the mountains

are the feet of those who bring

good news.

Isaiah 52:7

Come to me, all you who are weary
and burdened, and I will give
you rest.
Matthew 11:28

The Lord is my light and my

salvation, whom shall I fear?

The Lord is the stronghold of my life,

of whom shall I be afraid?

Psalm 27:1

Jesus Christ is the same

yesterday, today and forever.

Hebrews 13:8

Because of the Lord's great love

we are not consumed, for his

compassions never fail. They are

new every morning; great is

your faithfulness.

Lamentations 3:22-23

My grace is sufficient for you,

my power is made perfect

in weakness.

2 Corinthians 12:9

So we fix our eyes not on what is seen, but on what is unseen. For what is seen in temporary, but what is unseen is eternal.

2 Corinthians 4:18

Delight yourself in the Lord and
he will give you the desires of
your heart. Commit your way to
the Lord, trust in him and
he will do this.
Psalm 37:4-5

I have been crucified with Christ
and I no longer live, but Christ
lives in me.
Galatians 2:20

Do not merely listen to the
word, and so deceive yourselves.
Do what it says.

James 1:22

But the fruit of the spirit is love

joy, peace, patience, kindness,

goodness, faithfulness, gentleness and

self-control.

Galations 5:22

May the words of my mouth and
the meditation of my heart be
pleasing in your sight, O Lord, my
Rock and my Redeemer.

Psalm 19:14

Your word is a lamp unto my

feet and a light unto my path.

Psalm 119:105

I have hidden your word in my

heart that I might not sin

against you.

Psalm 119:11

Let us then approach the throne of grace with confidence, so that we may receive mercy and find grace to help us in our time of need.

Hebrews 4:16

If we confess our sins, he is faithful

and just and will forgive us our

sins and purify us from all

unrighteousness

1 John 1:9

Therefore confess your sins to each
other and pray for each other so
that you may be healed.

James 5:16

And what does the Lord require
of you? To act justly and to love
mercy and to walk humbly
with your God.

Micah 6:8

I tell you the truth, whatever you
did for one of the least of these
brothers of mine, you did for me.
Matthew 25:40

And surely I am with you always, to the very end of the age.

Matthew 28:20

The Lord will stand with you

and give you strength

1 Timothy 4:17

But as for you be strong and
don't give up, for your work
will be rewarded.

2 Chronicles 5:7

I loved you at your

darkest.

Romans 5:8

You've got someone standing beside you who is stronger than the one standing against you.

Joshua 1:5

Let all that you do be done

in love.

1 Corinthians 16:14

When you go through deep waters, I will be with you.

Isaiah 48:2

Be joyful in hope, patient in affliction and faithful in prayer.

Romans 12:12

But when you ask you must believe and not doubt, because the one who doubts is like a wave in the sea, blown and tossed in the wind.

James 1:6

He reached down from on high;

and took hold of me and drew

me out of deep waters.

2 Samuel 22:17

Now may the Lord of peace
himself give you peace at all times
and in every way.
to give you hope and a future"
2 Thessalonians 3:16

Let us not love with words or

speech but with actions and in truth.

1 John 3:18

He has made everything

beautiful in it's time.

Ecclesiastes 3:11

Rise up, take courage

and do it

Ezra 10:4

Whenever you feel unloved, unimportant or insecure remember to whom you belong.

Ephesians 2:19-22

The pain that you have been

feeling cannot compare to the

joy that is coming.

Romans 8:18

Love your enemies, do good to those who hate you, bless those who curse you, pray for those who mistreat you.

Luke 6:27-28

To everything there is a season,

a time for every purpose

under heaven.

Ecclesiastes 3:1

Give thanks to the Lord for
he is good, his love endures forever.
Psalm 106:9

God is our refuge and strength,

an ever present help in trouble.

Psalm 46:1

Let love and faithfulness never
leave you; bind them around your
neck, write them on the tablet
of your heart.
Proverbs 3:3

Greater love has no one than this,

then to lay down one's life

for his friends.

John 15:13

I can do all things through

Christ who gives me strength.

Philippians 4:13

Now faith is the assurance of things hoped for, the conviction of things not seen.

Hebrews 11:1

For he will put angels in charge

of you to guard you in all

your ways.

Psalm 91:11

Made in the USA
Coppell, TX
28 September 2023